2ND EDITION

A MODERN APPROACH TO CLASSICAL GUITAR

T0048401

By CHARLES DUNCAN

Book 2

Description	Page
Before You Begin	2
Tempo Markings	2
Interpretive Markings	3
Playing with Free Stroke	4
Open-String Free-Stroke Exercises	5
Giuliani's Arpeggio Exercises	6
Scale Construction	8
Key Signatures	9
Chord Construction	10
Barred Chords: The Half-Barre	11
Common Musical Styles and Textures	12
Etude 1	12
Etude 2	12
Etude 3	13
Etude 4	13
Etude 5	14
Etude 6	14
Etude 7	15
Etude 8	15
First Classical Solos	16
Andantino by M. Carcassi	16
Country Dance by F. Carulli	17
Accenting a Melody with Rest Strokes	18
Waltz by F. Carulli	18
Andante by F. Sor	19
What If a Day or a Month or a Year (anonymous)	20
Minuet by H. Purcell	21
Sixteenth Notes	22
Estudio in Am by D. Aguado	22
Dotted Eighth Notes	23
Moderato by F. Carulli	24
Andante by W. A. Mozart	25
Playing in 6/8 Time	26
Nocturne by C. Duncan	27
Barcarole by F. Carulli	28
Moderato by M. Giuliani	29
Interlude: Song Accompaniments	30
Michael, Row the Boat Ashore	30
Cockles and Mussels	31
Amazing Grace	32
Scarborough Fair	33
Syncopation	34
Hava Nagilah	34
Joshua Fought the Battle of Jericho	35
Position Playing: Second and Third Positions	36
Second-Position Etude	37
Third-Position Etude	38
Chorale by J. S. Bach	39
Bagatelle by R. Schumann	40
God Rest Ye Merry, Gentlemen	41
Using the Second and Third Position in Solos	42
Espanoleta by G. Sanz	42
Prelude in C by C. Duncan	43
Allemande (anonymous)	44
Bourreé by J. S. Bach	45
Bourreé by J. Krieger	45
Packington's Pound (anonymous)	46
Caprice by M. Carcassi	47
Left-Hand Technique: Using Slurs	48
Ascending Slurs ("Hammering on")	48
Descending Slurs ("Pulling off")	49
Minuet in G by J. S. Bach	50
Rondino by J. Ph. Rameau	51
Gratia d'Amore by F. Caroso	52
Alba Novella by F. Caroso	53
Für Elise by L. van Beethoven	54
Using Slurs for Ornamentation	55
The Grace Note	55
The Double Grace Note	55
Andante by F. Sor	56
Etude by M. Giuliani	57
Coda: Spanish Music in the Phrygian Mode	58
Fiesta by C. Duncan	59
Malagueña (arr. C. Duncan)	60
Appendix: Playing with Fingernails	62
Filing the Nails	62
Shaping the Nails	63
Playing with the Thumbnail	64

ISBN 978-0-7935-7071-3

HAL•LEONARD® CORPORATION

7777 W. BLUEMOUND RD. P.O. BOX 13819 MILWAUKEE, WI 53213

In Australia Contact:
Hal Leonard Australia Pty. Ltd.
4 Lentara Court
Cheltenham, Victoria, 3192 Australia
Email: ausadmin@halleonard.com.au

Copyright © 2012 by HAL LEONARD CORPORATION
International Copyright Secured All Rights Reserved

No part of this publication may be reproduced in any form or by any means without the prior written permission of the Publisher.

Visit Hal Leonard Online at
www.halleonard.com

Before You Begin…

If you've mastered the skills developed in *Book 1* of this series, you're ready to move up to a more advanced level of classical guitar playing. In this book, you'll be learning a lot of new skills—see page 1 for an overview of what they are. You'll also begin exploring the classical guitar repertoire, with over two dozen pieces chosen for their superior musical quality as well as some of the author's own compositions. Since the use of right-hand fingernails is usually recommended for students at this level, a thorough discussion of nail usage is included as an appendix (pp. 62–64).

You'll use this book to best advantage along with its companion volumes *A Modern Approach to Classical Guitar Repertoire, Part 1* (second edition, 2009) and *Easy Classical Guitar Duets*. Besides the enjoyable and progressively more difficult pieces, the accompanying CDs will give you a good idea of how much beauty can be found in the easy-to-intermediate repertoire.

Students at this level should also recognize and begin using the interpretive terms and symbols that are usually incorporated into classical guitar music. You'll see them throughout this book; the following two sections provide a handy reference guide to their meaning.

✔ **TIP:** It's also a good idea to have a basic music dictionary in your personal book collection. The *Hal Leonard Pocket Music Dictionary* is a handy and inexpensive option.

TEMPO MARKINGS

Composers and music editors use a variety of tempo terms to indicate the speed at which a piece should be played. Since Italian is the international language of classical music, they're usually in Italian. From slowest to fastest, the most common ones are the following:

Grave	Slow and solemn
Largo	Slow and stately
Lento	Slow but with a lighter emotional tone
Adagio	Slow but with a stronger rhythmic flow
Larghetto	Somewhat faster and lighter in mood
Andante	At an easy, walking pace
Andantino	Somewhat faster than Andante
Moderato	At a moderately brisk pace
Allegretto	Fairly fast; light and charming
Allegro	Fast and joyful
Presto	Very fast
Prestissimo	As fast as possible

A more objective measure of tempo is the **metronome setting** that sometimes appears along with the tempo marking; you'll see it used throughout this book for all the pieces. Look for the abbreviation **M.M.** followed by the number of beats per minute. (The abbreviation M.M. stands for "Maelzel's Metronome" in honor of Johann Maelzel, the 19th century inventor of the metronome.) For example, a metronome setting of M.M. ♩=80 tells you to set the metronome to click (or pulse) at 80 BPM, and then play along with the beats to get the feel of the correct tempo. Electronic metronomes from $25–$50 are available at most music stores.

INTERPRETIVE MARKINGS

You'll also be seeing a number of interpretive markings, most often in the form of abbreviations or symbols. These are used to guide the player's control of rhythm and dynamics in order to interpret the music with feeling and good musicianship. The most common are the following:

Abbreviation	Italian Term	Meaning
p; pp	*piano; pianissimo*	soft; very soft
mp	*mezzo piano*	rather soft
mf	*mezzo forte*	moderately loud
f; ff	*forte; fortissimo*	loud; very loud
sfz	*sforzando*	suddenly louder
acc. or >	*accento*	play with an accent
dim. or >	*diminuendo*	getting softer
cresc. or <	*crescendo*	getting louder
accel.	*accelerando*	speeding up
rit.	*ritardando*	slowing down
rall.	*rallentando*	gradually fading away
espr.	*espressivo*	expressively; with feeling
𝄐	*fermata*	hold for longer than the literal note value

In addition, terms such as the following are used without abbreviations or symbols:

animato	lively; with animation
con moto	with a strong sense of rhythmic drive
maestoso	with majestic feeling
affetuoso	with tender feeling
poco; molto	a little; very much
a tempo (after a ***rit.*** or ***accel.***)	play at the original tempo

Of course, when you're learning to play a piece, you must always practice much slower than the indicated metronome setting, and you needn't be concerned with the fine points of interpretation. However, once you've mastered the technical requirements of a piece, practicing it for control of rhythm and dynamics will provide even more enjoyment. If you're interested in playing for people, this kind of practice will also help develop the kind of professionalism and emotional warmth that listeners expect.

Playing with Free Stroke

Except for scales and accented notes, most classical guitar playing past the beginner level is based on the **free stroke**, which enables you to play chords, arpeggios, and counterpoint. To play with free stroke, you'll need to keep your wrist and forearm a little higher than for rest stroke. For most players, the best position is around three inches from the top of the guitar.

Notice that the wrist is only slightly arched, and that the knuckles are fairly high, positioned almost directly over the fingertips. This allows space for your fingers to escape the strings toward the palm of the hand while you maintain a strong, natural right-hand position.

You should avoid flattening the knuckles and curling the fingers, because this creates tension in the hand and tends to produce poor string tone. When positioned correctly, the fingers should escape the strings at a fairly shallow angle, as shown in the first illustration.

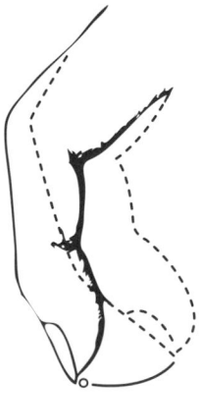

Right

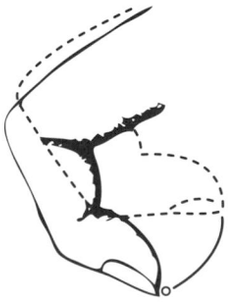

Wrong

✔ **TIP:** You can think of a good free stroke as a modified rest stroke. As the illustrations indicate, the correct finger motion is actually more like a down-and-in push than a strictly upward pluck.

Open-String Free-Stroke Exercises

Practice the following open-string chordal exercises slowly and carefully to get the feel of free-stroke playing. In the first one, place your thumb on the fifth string for support. If you're playing with nails, pay close attention to how the nails engage the strings.

TIP: It's like notching, drawing, and releasing an arrow—the "arrow" being the resulting tone.

Now try adding the thumb. If the opposed movement of the thumb and fingers seems a bit awkward at first, just experiment with your touch until you can produce clean-sounding chords.

Now try a couple of basic **arpeggio** exercises.

TIP: "Plant" your fingernails (or fingertips) on the strings at the beginning of each measure, just as if you were going to play a four-note chord. The technique of **planting** helps develop secure touch and can be used whenever notes of an arpeggio are in an ascending direction. Also, the doubling of the bass notes does not mean that they are played twice! This is merely a device used in arpeggiated music to indicate the actual duration of the bass note which supports the arpeggio.

Giuliani's Arpeggio Exercises

Mauro Giuliani (1781–1839), one of the great guitar composers, wrote numerous excellent short pieces for students. You'll be playing some of them very soon, but a few of his *120 Studies for the Right Hand*, which are comparable to the famous Hanon and Czerny exercises for piano, will complete your basic introduction to free-stroke playing. Besides being fun to practice, these exercises will develop your technical skill while you're studying the more theoretical material on the next four pages. Thereafter, they can serve as useful daily warm-up exercises.

Each exercise is based on a simple alternation between the C and G7 chords shown below, along with the corresponding chord diagrams. (Memorize and practice until you can make the chord changes easily before attempting the exercises.)

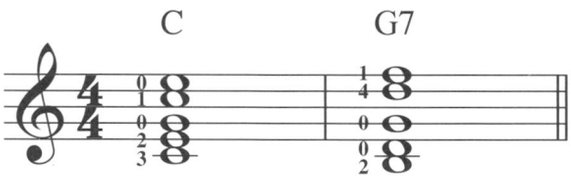

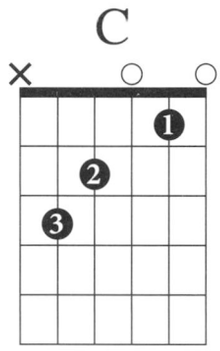

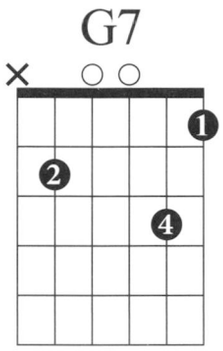

Notice also that these exercises are written in **eighth-note triplets**. The eighth-note triplet is used to subdivide a beat into thirds in 2/4, 3/4, and 4/4 and is very easy to count. You can count triplets by saying either "one-trip-let, two-trip-let," etc., or "one-and-a, two-and-a," etc., as shown below:

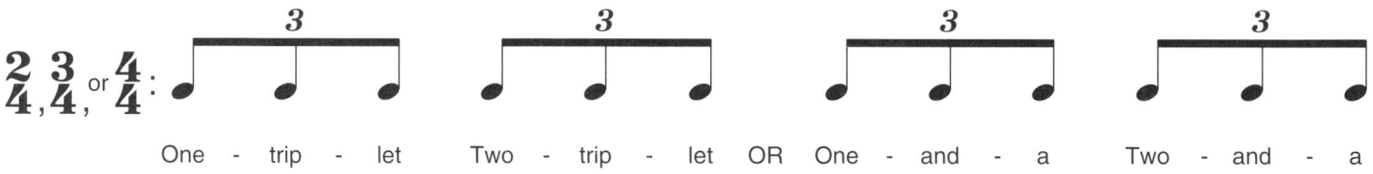

Practice these exercises slowly and carefully. Play each exercise at least twice, concluding with the final C chord.

TIP: Look for opportunities to practice planting the ascending notes of an arpeggio whenever you see the fingerings *p–i–m*, *p–i–a*, or *p–i–m–a*.

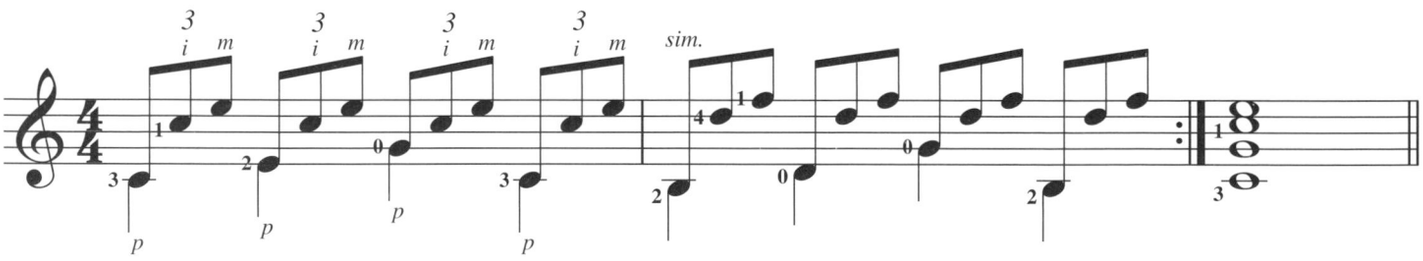

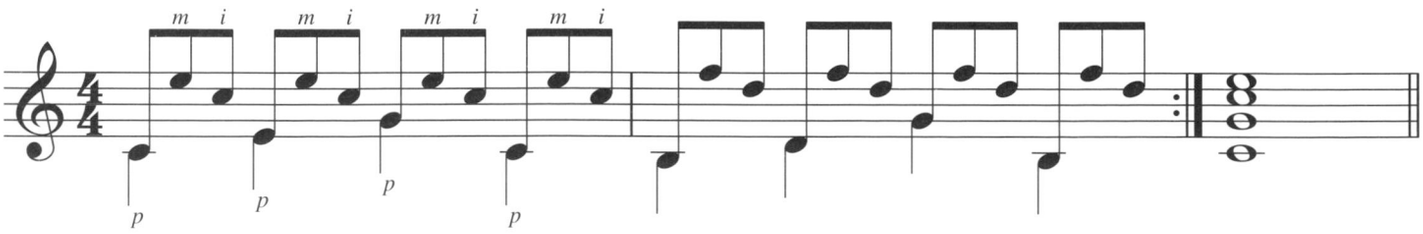

i a i m i a i m
p p p p

a i m i a i m i
p p p p

i m a m i i m i m
p p p

m i a m i m i m i
p p p

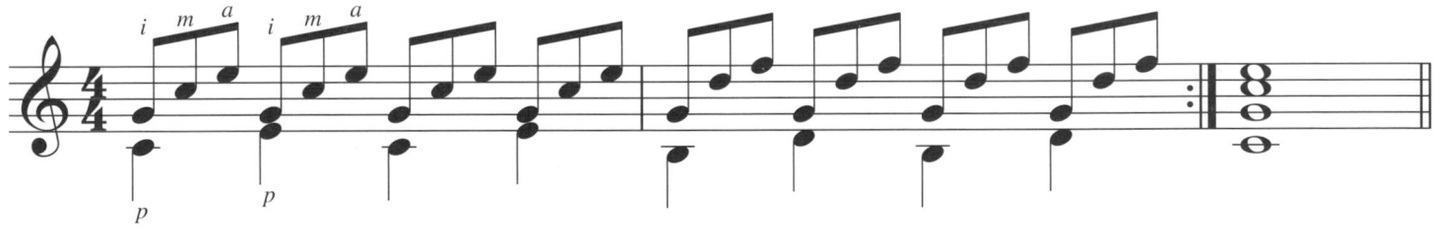
i m a i m a
p p

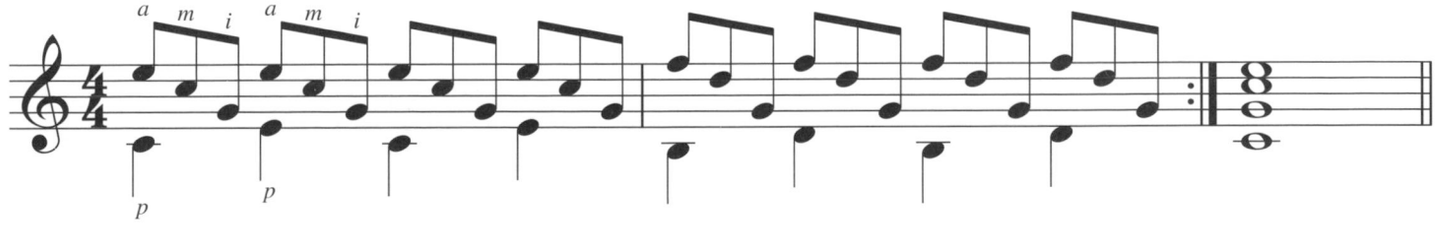
a m i a m i
p p

Scale Construction

You'll need to practice the preceding exercises for a while before you move on. In the meantime, let's pause for a look at some basic music theory, beginning with how scales are constructed. In this section, you'll also learn an important new left-hand technique: the **half-barre** (or half-bar).

The most common scales in classical music are the **major** and **minor diatonic scales**, composed of seven scale tones (or scale degrees) with a specific pattern of **half steps** and **whole steps**. On the guitar, a half step is the musical distance between notes on neighboring frets; a whole step is the musical distance between notes separated by a fret.

For all major scales, the pattern of half and whole steps is the same as for the C major scale shown below (**W**=whole step, **H**=half step):

Major

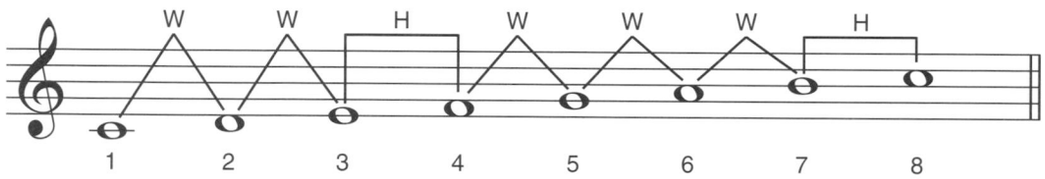

For all minor scales, the pattern is the same as for the A minor scales below. However, minor scales are a bit more complicated. Notice that there are three of them: the natural minor, the harmonic minor, and the melodic minor. The natural minor is the foundation, while the harmonic minor raises the 7th degree by a half step.

Natural minor

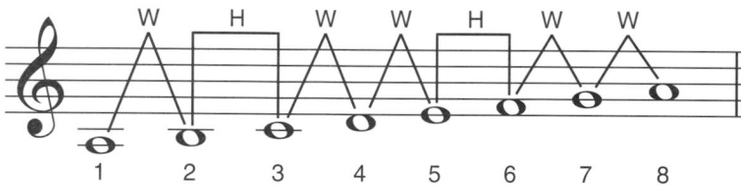

Harmonic minor

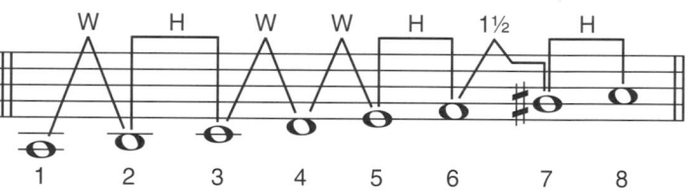

The chords in minor keys are based on the harmonic minor scale. However, since the raised 7th creates an awkward 1½ step melodic interval between scale degrees 6 and 7, for melodies in minor keys the melodic minor is preferred. The melodic minor uses both a raised 6th and 7th degree ascending; when descending, it uses the natural 6th and 7th degrees.

Melodic minor

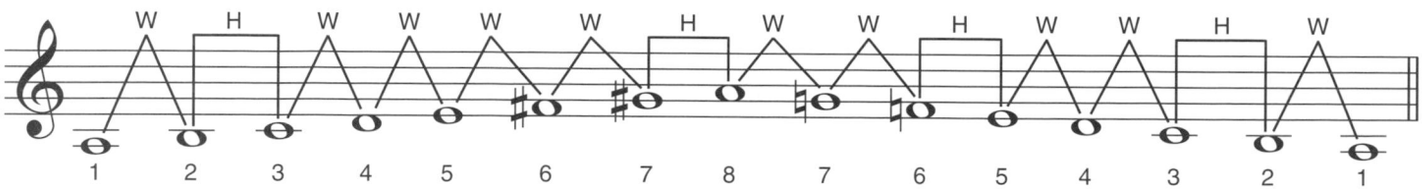

Key Signatures

In order to keep the correct pattern of half and whole steps, all major and minor scales (except C and Am) require a **chromatic alteration**. The number of sharps or flats needed to produce the correct pattern of intervals also designates the **musical key** that the scale defines. The key is indicated by a **key signature** at the beginning of each line of music, consisting of one to six sharps or flats—for example:

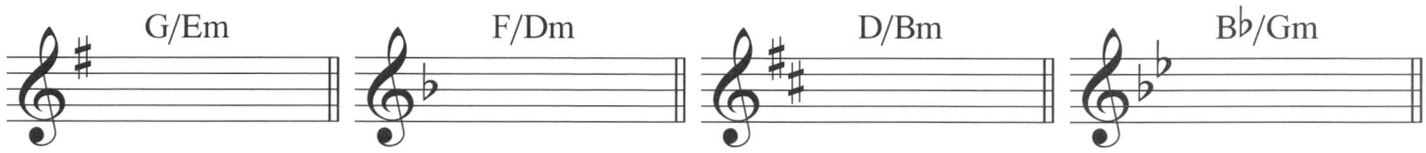

Most music for the classical guitar is written in keys with no more than four sharps or two flats. Because of the abundance of good pieces in C and Am and G and Em (one sharp), in this book you'll only need to recognize the first key signature above. (*Book 3* will provide a progressive introduction to music in the other principal keys.)

To learn all the first-position notes in the new keys of G and Em, memorize and practice the following two-octave scales, using the *m–i* rest stroke. To continue improving the strength and coordination of the *a* finger, practice with *a–i* and *a–m* rest stroke as well.

✔ **TIP:** Remember that *all* the Fs are sharped—look for the reminder sharps over the lower-octave Fs.

G Major

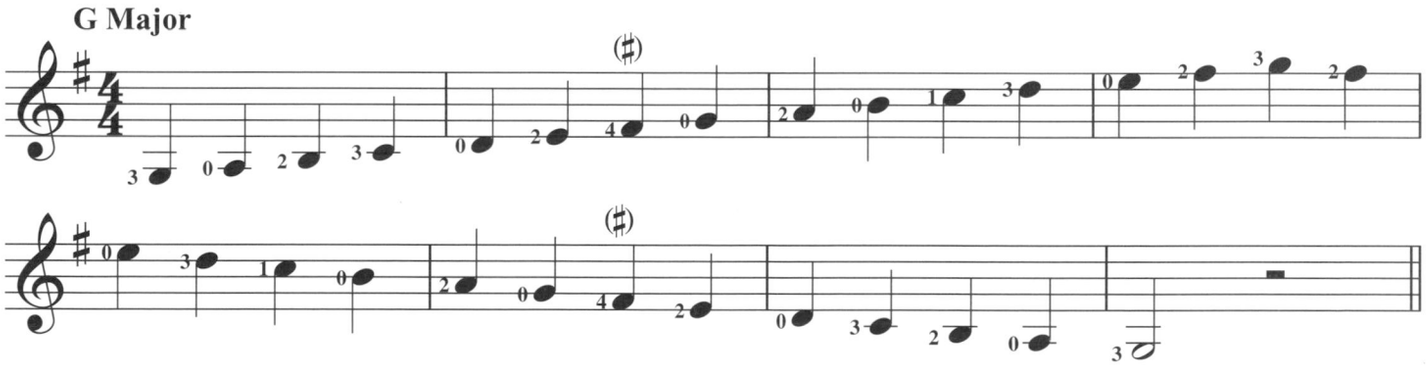

E Melodic minor

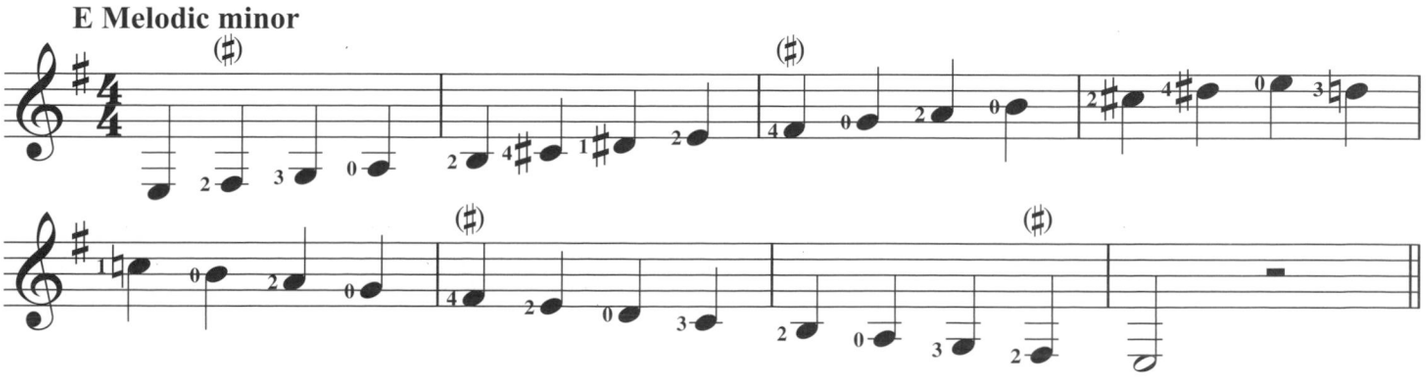

Chord Construction

All chords are composed of the intervals defined by major and minor diatonic scales, as shown below for the C scale. The interval from scale tone one (the **root**) to scale tone two is a **second**, from the root to scale tone three a **third**, and so on up the scale.

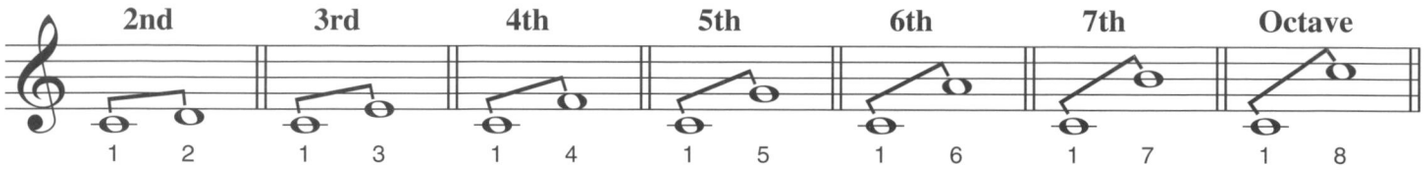

Any of these intervals may appear in major, minor, or seventh chords, depending on how the chords are **voiced**. However, **stacked thirds** are the basis of chord construction. Two stacked thirds produce a **triad**, containing both the third and fifth tones above the root. The common guitar chord is derived by doubling and rearranging the triad tones, as shown below for the C and D minor chords:

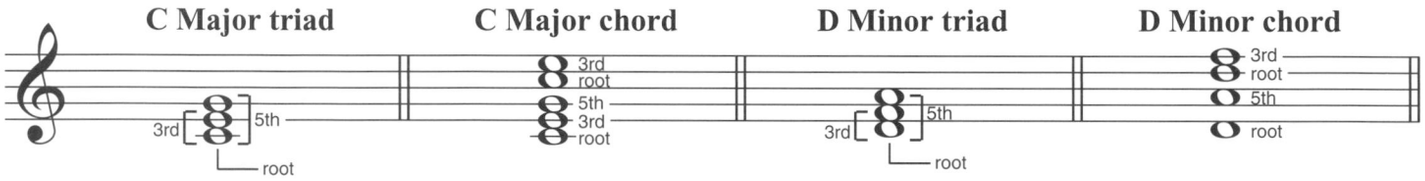

When three thirds are stacked, the resulting chord is called a **seventh** chord, because the interval between the root and the highest note is a seventh. However, you'll very seldom see seventh chords in this form in guitar music. Because of the way the instrument is tuned, you'll usually see them in a more **open voicing**, as shown below for G7 and E7 chords:

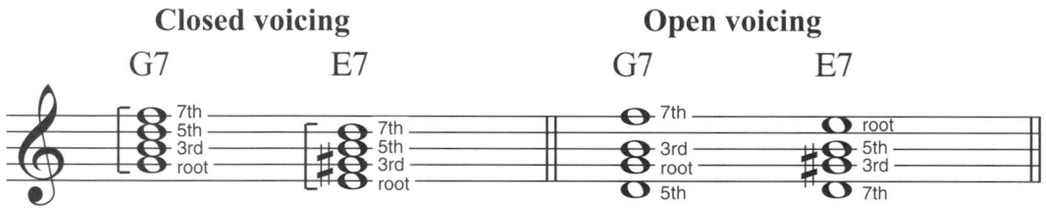

The chords build on the first, fourth, and fifth notes of the scale are known as **primary chords**, because they provide the basic harmonic skeleton of most classical and popular music. Respectively, they're called the **tonic**, **subdominant**, and **dominant** chords, and the dominant is often a seventh chord. They can also be designated by Roman numerals as **I**, **IV**, and **V(7)**. Although you'll usually play them in more formal voicings, you should memorize the common primary chords for the keys of A minor, G, and E minor.

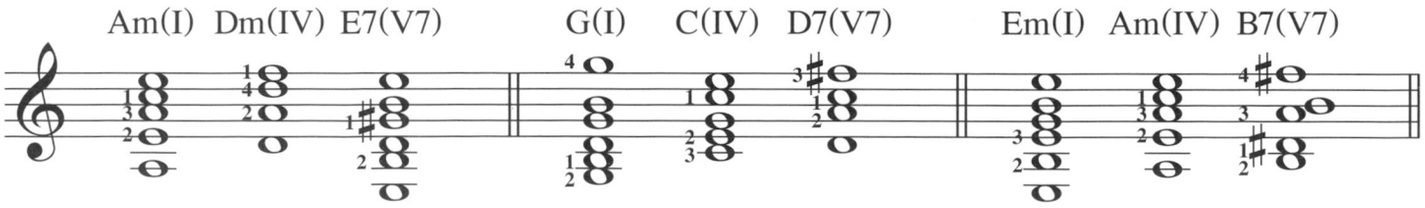

Barred Chords: The Half-Barre

The primary chords for the key of C major are C, F, and G7. Look closely at the fingering shown for the F chord. To play the F chord, you'll need to learn an important new left-hand technique—the **half-barre**, indicated here by the bracket in the music and the curved line in the corresponding chord.

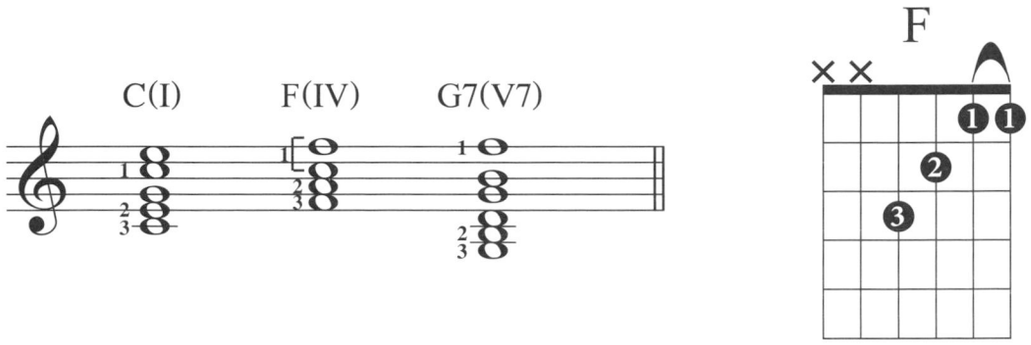

In this book, you'll be using the half-barre from time to time, so start practicing it now; it takes time to develop the necessary strength and coordination. Also, you'll be developing the kind of skill needed for the **full barre**, which is introduced in *Book 3*.

To make the half-barre, flatten the finger from the middle joint to the tip as shown below in the first photograph.

TIP: The knuckle should be sharply bent so that it can exert the necessary leverage from above. Leverage from below is provided by the thumb, which opposes the first finger as shown in the second photo.

Now memorize and practice the following two **cadences** in the key of C major. Cadences are I–IV–V7–I progressions that use the kind of voicing common to classical music. Each note of the chord can be considered a separate voice, as in four-part vocal harmony. Notice also the ¢ over the F chord. In most guitar music, the symbol for the half-barre is ¢ or ½ C (for *ceja*, the Spanish word for "bar"), followed by the fret number in either Arabic or Roman numerals.

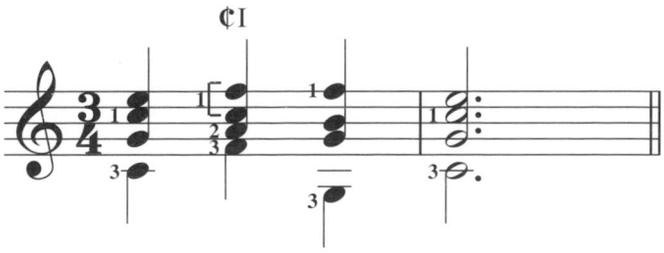

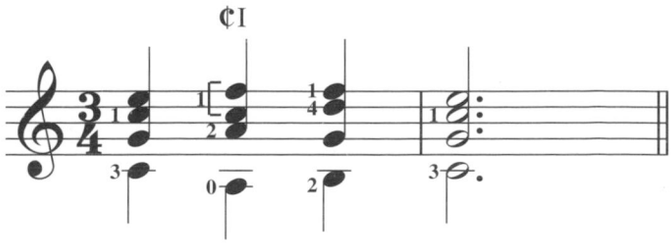

Common Musical Styles and Textures

Several musical styles and textures are so common in classical guitar music that you'll benefit from learning them before trying to learn the solos that begin on page 16. Practicing the etudes in this section will also help train your fingers for the kinds of coordination needed to play the solos.

Notice that the etudes are based harmonically on the use of **consonant intervals**, which are the foundation of traditional harmony. Consonant intervals are those that sound naturally pleasing to the ear—especially **thirds**, **sixths**, and **tenths**. The tenth has the same harmonic quality as the third, but with an additional octave between the higher and lower notes.

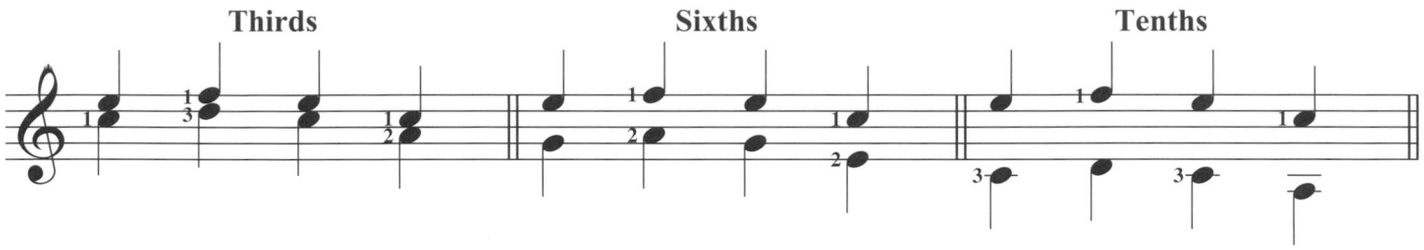

ETUDE 1—Simple two-part harmony, using primarily thirds and sixths. Play with *i–m*.

ETUDE 2—Simple two-part harmony, using only parallel sixths. **Parallel harmony** is the parallel movement of two or more voices. Play the melody using alternate *m–i* free strokes.

ETUDE 3—Simple three-part harmony based primarily on parallel tenths with an **internal pedal point**. The term "pedal point" refers to the way organists can sustain a bass note indefinitely with a foot pedal. This style of arpeggiated harmony was popularized by the composer Domenico Alberti (1710–1740) and is also known as **Alberti bass**. Guitar composers of the period 1770–1850 used this style very frequently.

ETUDE 4—Somewhat more complex three-part harmony, with movement primarily in thirds supported by an independent bass line. This too is a very typical kind of texture you'll be seeing more of. Use *p–i–m* throughout.

✔ **TIP:** The thumb always plays the bass line (the downstemmed notes).

ETUDE 5—Four-part harmony, with a simple melody supported by **block chords**. Listen carefully for the melody, and be sure that the *a* finger plays with as much force as *i* and *m*.

✔ **TIP:** You'll find that it helps to compress the right-hand fingers together—the more compact the hand, the more solid the stroke of the *a* finger. Note also the key signature; the etude is in E minor, and all the Fs are sharped.

ETUDE 6—Melody and bass combined in simple two-part **counterpoint**. In this kind of texture, the bass line provides a firm harmonic foundation for the independent movement of the melody. In pieces of this kind, the right-hand fingering can be tricky. Just practice slowly and carefully.

In each of the preceding etudes, the highest voice is the melody. However, the melody can also be in the bass, as seen in the two arpeggio etudes on the next page. Try to accent the bass notes and be sure to give them their full time value, as indicated by the double note values and downstems.

ETUDE 7—This etude uses the F chord, indicated by the ¢ over the measures where it is used. Also, remember that the downstem half notes are *not* to be played as separate notes. This form of notation is used only to indicate the actual duration of the bass notes.

ETUDE 8—Notice the key signature and the repeat of the first line of music. Notice also the tied notes at the end. In the last measure, you play only the fourth-string E; the other notes of the E major chord carry over from the preceding measure.

First Classical Solos

These paired compositions by Matteo Carcassi (1792–1853) and Ferdinand Carulli (1770–1841) make a good introduction to solo playing. Both are fairly easy as well as fun to play, and both illustrate the style and texture of guitar music from the **Classical period** in music (approximately 1770–1850). Music from this period tends to be very symmetrically constructed, with a melody supported by broken chords as in Etude 3.

Carcassi's simple but effective structure is based on the repetition of two complete musical thoughts. Carulli's structure is somewhat more complex, with a contrasting third section and a **da capo**, indicated by the **D.C. al Fine** at the end. "Da Capo al Fine" means "play again from the beginning to the end *without repeats*." Whenever you see this term, go back to the beginning and play up to the **Fine**, which indicates the actual ending of the piece.

Andantino

Matteo Carcassi

Country Dance

TRACK 16

Accenting a Melody with Rest Strokes

Good players often use rest strokes to provide melodic accent in pieces such as the "Waltz" below, especially for notes on the first string. For second-string notes, the **half rest stroke** is usually preferred. A half rest stroke is a free stroke with a heavier downward push into the string. With practice, you'll discover that it can sound almost identical to a rest stroke. Practice the following pattern study with *a–m* rest strokes to get the general feel of this kind of touch.

Carulli's charming little "Waltz" also illustrates another way Alberti bass can be written, using upstems instead of downstems for the internal pedal tone. Consequently, the piece looks like an arpeggio exercise, but the notes on strings 1 and 2 provide a distinct melody. See the accent marks (>) in the first line of music.

Waltz

Ferdinand Carulli

Allegretto M.M. ♩ = 104

Fernando Sor (1778–1839) was one of the very best classical guitar composers; in fact, he's been called the Beethoven of the guitar. The piece below is a good example of the many beautiful compositions he wrote for students.

More complex melodies, such as the one in this piece, offer more opportunities for variety of accent. To begin, try to use rest strokes or half rest strokes for the notes indicated by accent marks. Then experiment with your touch to see where else similar accents might sound good.

✔ **TIP:** The overall effect should be a lyrical, flowing melody with lots of tonal color.

Andante

The following two pieces will introduce you to the musical styles and textures of the **Renaissance period** (approximately 1550–1650) and the **Baroque period** (approximately 1660–1750).

"What If a Day or a Month or a Year" is an anonymous instrumental version of a song by Thomas Campion, an English poet of the period. It's a good example of the kind of music composed for the **lute**, which was the most popular instrument of the Renaissance. Because the lute is so similar to the guitar, most lute music can be played without alteration on the classical guitar.

This piece is also fairly easy to play, except for the shift to the B major chord in the third line. Since the chord contains a somewhat difficult spacing of *p–i–m–a*, you'll need to practice this shift separately.

✔ **TIP:** To help make the shift secure for the left hand, be sure to use the fourth finger as a **guide finger** (as indicated by the dash).

What If a Day or a Month or a Year

Anonymous
16th century English

Henry Purcell was the finest English composer of the Baroque period, and the *minuet* was one of the most popular dances of the 17th and 18th centuries. Written for harpsichord, the forerunner of the modern piano, this charming little piece is a good example of the kind of **transcriptions** that are an important part of the classical guitar repertoire. (A transcription is an adaptation of a piece written for another instrument.) Since it's based primarily on simple two-part counterpoint, it's also fairly easy to play, except for a few difficult fingerings in the third line.

✔ **TIP:** Practice the third line separately as an exercise. (Practicing the more difficult passages separately is always a good idea.)

Minuet

Henry Purcell

Andantino M.M. ♩ = 112

mf

mp

f

mf

poco rit.

Sixteenth Notes

When the quarter note is divided by fourths, the result is a **sixteenth note** (i.e., one-sixteenth of a whole note). Single sixteenth notes are written with a double flag; groups of sixteenth notes are written with a double beam: A sixteenth rest looks the same as an eighth rest, but with a double tail:

Groups of four sixteenth notes are counted "one-e-and-a, two-e-and-a," etc. Practice the following rhythm line with an *i–m* rest stroke, counting aloud as shown.

The following beneficial arpeggio study also provides an easy introduction to reading music written in sixteenth notes. Like Carulli, Giuliani, and Sor, Dionisio Aguado (1784–1849) was another fine guitar composer of the early 19th century who wrote many well-known short study pieces.

This piece also introduces you to the use of **position shifting** to simplify the left-hand fingering. You'll learn more about position shifting later in the book. For now, you'll enjoy using the easy shifts in the first line of music.

TIP: In the first line of music, note the use of guide fingers. Note also the circled string number ③, which indicates that you play the B in measure 3 on the third string.

Estudio in Am

Dionisio Aguado

Allegretto M.M. ♩ = 72

i m i

p *p* ③

mf

f

Two sixteenth notes can also be beamed together with an eighth note as shown: Count this **rhythmic figure** by saying "one—and-a, two—and-a," etc., as in the rhythm line below. Practice with *m–i* rest strokes while counting aloud.

In the famous "Lone Ranger" theme from the William Tell Overture, this figure is used as a **rhythmic motive** (a motive is a short musical idea). Practice with *m–i* rest strokes while counting aloud.

Dotted Eighth Notes

A dot after an eighth note increases its value by half: = + The dotted eighth note is usually beamed with a sixteenth note to create another kind of rhythmic figure—**dotted eighths and sixteenths:** A good way to learn this figure is to practice the dotted eighth as if it were three tied sixteenths, as in the rhythm line below. Be sure to count aloud.

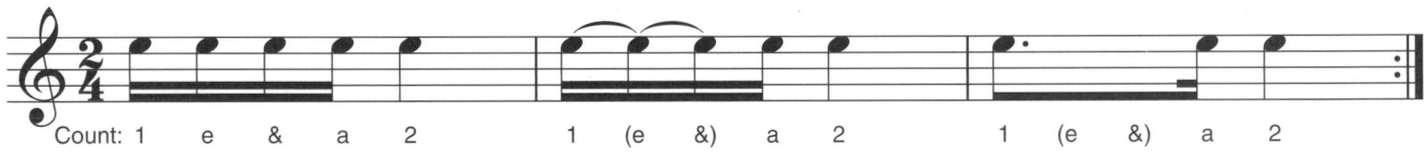

The "Battle Hymn of the Republic" is an excellent example of the use of dotted eighths and sixteenths. Practice with *i–m* rest strokes while counting aloud.

✔ **TIP:** Although the sixteenth note is beamed with the *preceding* downbeat, it is actually an **upbeat** to the *next* downbeat. Listen for this strong rhythmic connection as you count "a-*one*, a-*two*," etc.

Carulli's "Moderato" has a much more varied texture and complex appearance than Aguado's "Estudio." However, it's easier to count and play than it appears at first sight.

TIP: If the rhythmic coordination of the bass and treble parts in the second line seems confusing, try counting aloud as you play. You'll see that the beat is evenly subdivided between the bass and treble, and each right hand finger-stroke matches the appropriate syllable of the "one-e-and-a, two-e-and-a" count.

Moderato

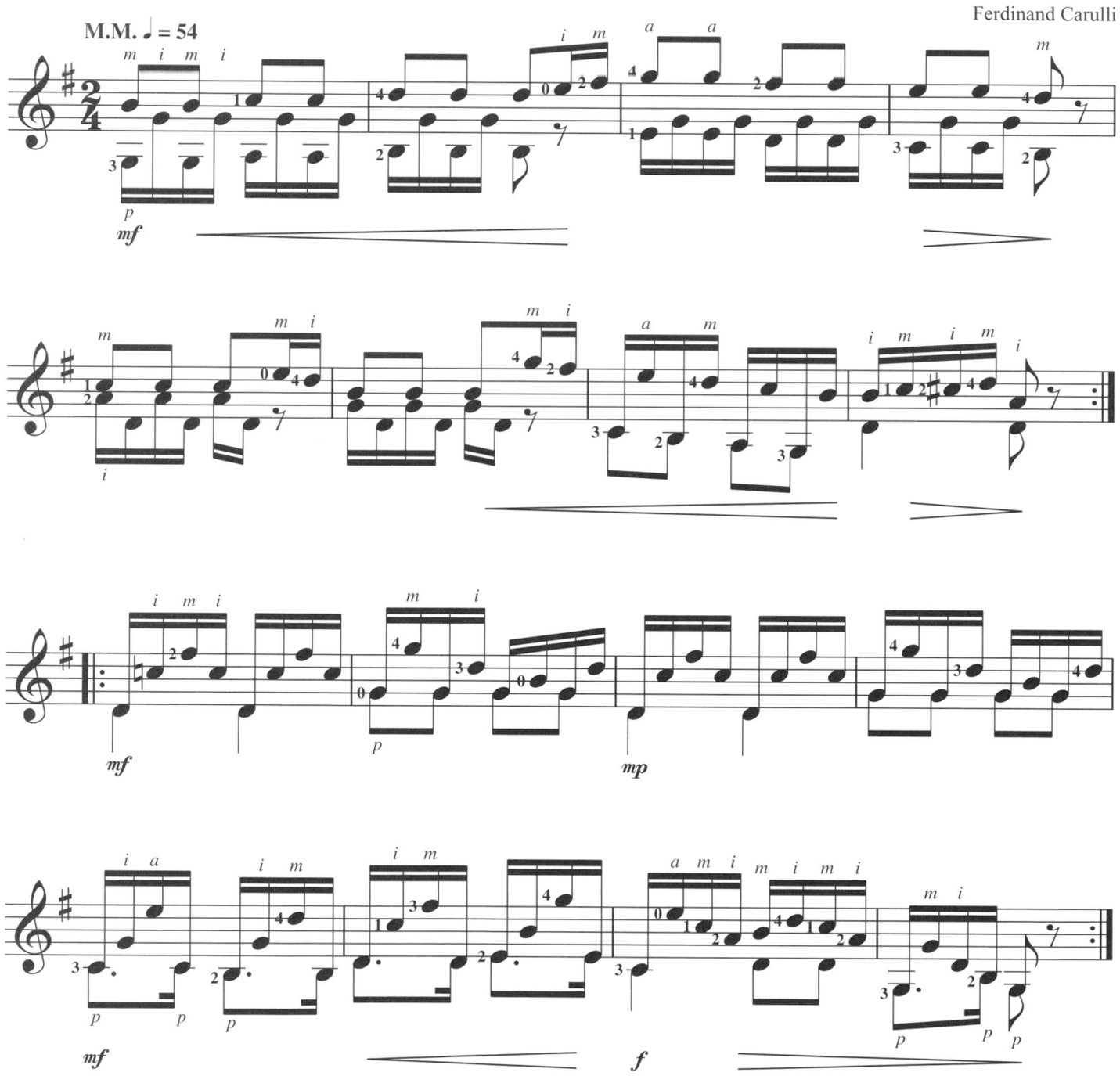

The following piece uses each division of the beat by sixteenth notes that you've learned to help create a strong melody with rhythmic variety. It's also a good example of the kind of highly original and lyrical music that Wolfgang Amadeus Mozart was writing for the piano well before the age of ten. The first measure in the second line is a bit tricky, but otherwise the piece is not difficult to play. Once you've mastered the rhythm, practice it for dynamic control to bring out the phrase shapes and song quality of the melody.

Andante

Playing in 6/8 Time

Until now, you've played music with time signatures based on the quarter note. Time signatures based on the eighth note include **3/8, 4/8, 6/8, 9/8,** and **12/8**. The most common of these is **6/8**. In 6/8 time, there are six beats to the measure, and all note and rest values are proportionate to the eighth note: ♪ 𝄾 = 1 beat, ♩ 𝄿 = 2 beats, and ♩. 𝄿· = 3 beats. Practice the rhythm line below slowly while counting aloud:

For 6/8 music in a slow tempo, or when practicing slowly, you should simply count "1-2-3-4-5-6," as in the classic French love song, "Plaisir d'Amour."

Plaisir d'Amour

However, when 6/8 is played at a faster tempo, there is an even more obvious "feel" of two strong beats to the measure than in "Plaisir d'Amour" (beats 1 and 4). In this case, it's more convenient to count "one-and-a, two-and-a," similar to the eighth-note triplets in the Giuliani arpeggio studies. A good example is this famous Irish jig:

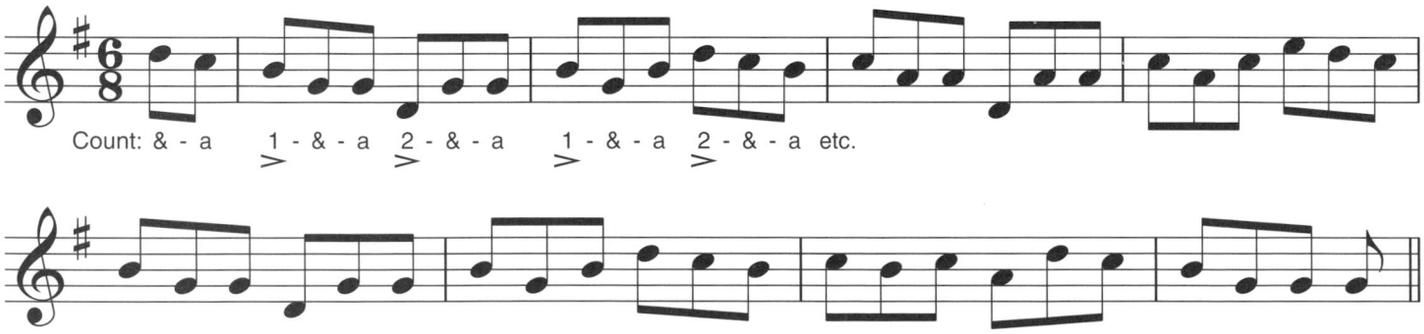

"Nocturne," on the next page, reflects the style of the 19th century Romantic composers such as Chopin, Beethoven, and Schumann who popularized the lyrical, dreamy *nocturne* form (the term means "night music"). The **Romantic period** in music is approximately 1800–1880; probably the most famous nocturne of all time is the first section of Beethoven's "Moonlight Sonata."

Nocturne

Charles Duncan

Carulli's "Barcarole" is a good example of another form used by composers to capture a lyrical, romantic mood. A *barcarole* (from Italian *barca*, meaning "boat") is a Venetian gondolier's song.

TIP: Look closely at the first line of music; the broken curved line means that you leave the first finger down as a **pivot** to anchor the hand and prevent unnecessary finger movement. Try to use this technique throughout the piece wherever the same musical figure appears.

Barcarole

Ferdinand Carulli

Giuliani wrote many charming miniature pieces to serve as etudes; the piece below is a good example. It introduces you to a somewhat more complex musical texture in 6/8 time, and the last line is a technical challenge in itself.

TIP: Practice the chord changes used in the last line in the form of the following cadence:

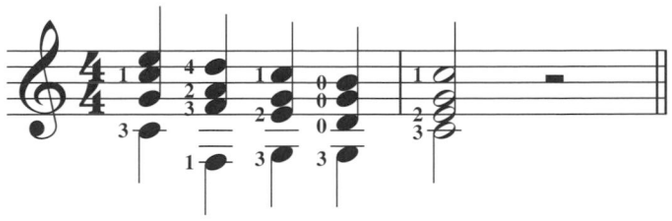

After you've mastered the technical challenges, practice for phrasing and melodic emphasis—try to make the piece "sing."

Moderato

Mauro Giuliani

M.M. ♩. = 52

mf *mp* *mf* *p*

Interlude: Song Accompaniments

While you're mastering the solos on the preceding pages, let's take a time-out for some enjoyable and beneficial recreational practice. If you don't already have some accompaniment skills, this section will be especially helpful.

The most widespread use of the guitar is as an accompaniment instrument, and well-rounded classical guitarists are very good at accompanying songs. The songs in this section will introduce you to the basic accompaniment styles for songs in 4/4 and 3/4, as well as provide further practice in playing arpeggios, changing chords, and using the half-barre F chord. If you're interested in developing your accompaniment skills further, several excellent Hal Leonard folk song and popular music anthologies are available.

Michael, Row the Boat Ashore

American Folk Song

Cockles and Mussels

Irish Ballad

Amazing Grace

Traditional Hymn

* The wavy vertical line is the symbol for a **broken chord**, also known as a **rolled chord**. Play it either with a brush stroke with the thumb, or a rapidly executed arpeggio with a double thumb stroke: *p p i ma.*

Scarborough Fair

Traditional English Ballad

Syncopation

The melodies of the following two pieces will also reinforce your knowledge of **syncopation**, which was introduced in *Book 1*. Syncopation occurs when normally unstressed beats or parts of a beat are rhythmically stressed. For example, in syncopated melodies, you'll often see quarter notes on an upbeat instead of the downbeat, or eighth notes tied to the next downbeat.

TIP: Whenever you see this kind of notation, remember that you'll need to play on the "ands" of the count.

Practice the two rhythm lines below, counting aloud. Then practice the melody part as well as the accompaniment part to "Hava Nagilah" and "Joshua Fought the Battle of Jericho." (Be sure to count aloud while learning the melody part.)

Hava Nagilah

Israeli Folk Dance

Joshua Fought the Battle of Jericho

American Spiritual

Position Playing: Second and Third Positions

Position playing is the term that guitarists use for playing beyond the first position on the fingerboard, with the fret played by the *first* finger as the reference point. For example, in **second position**, your first finger plays the *2nd* fret notes, and therefore you can play notes as high as the 5th fret without moving your hand. Similarly, in **third position**, you can play notes as high as the 6th fret without moving your hand, and so on up the fingerboard. You'll learn more about position playing in *Book 3*. For now, a good command of second- and third-position playing is enough, since most of the easy-to-intermediate classical guitar repertoire doesn't use notes past the 6th or 7th frets.

When you're playing in second or third position, open-string and 1st-fret notes are played on *the next lower string*, as shown below for the notes that you'll be playing in their next higher fingerboard positions.

✔ **TIP:** This pattern of repetition up on the fingerboard is known as the **rule of five frets**—any note on strings 1, 3, 4, and 5 can also be found five frets higher up on the fingerboard on the next lower string. Second-string notes are found *four* frets higher on the third string.

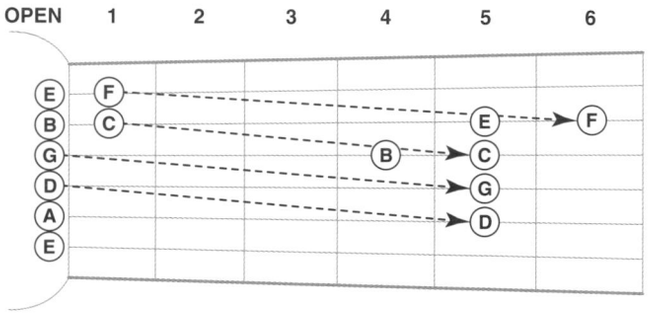

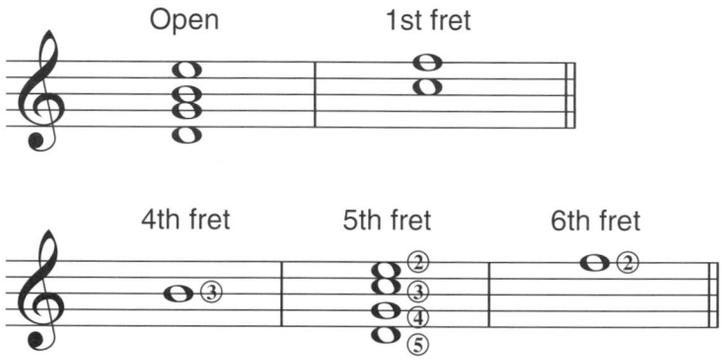

To learn the second- and third-position notes that you'll be playing, practice the following scale pattern exercises. When you're comfortable with the exercises, go on to the duets on the next five pages.

G Major, second position

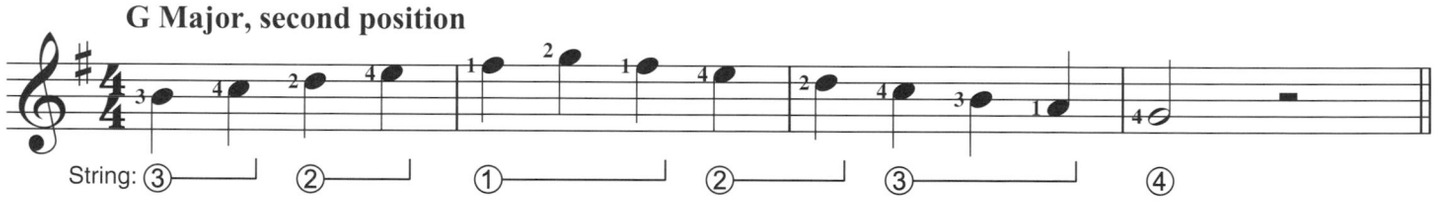

C Major, third position

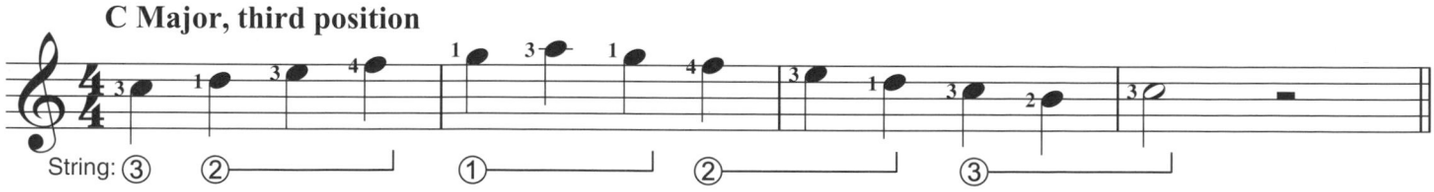

A Melodic minor, second and third position

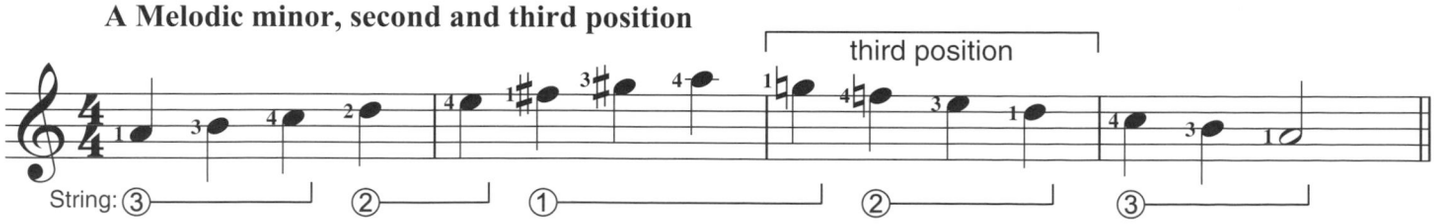

The following two etudes by the author in contrasting pop music styles will give you an easy introduction to playing in second and third position. They also illustrate the more advanced kind of accompaniment skills that you'll be capable of at a higher level of guitaristic development. Practice each melody slowly and carefully, using the position fingerings shown. For the accompaniment you can have an instructor play with you.

Second-Position Etude

Third-Position Etude

The melody of this slow, majestic piece by J.S. Bach is played entirely in second position. Even though it is a rather quiet piece, use good, solid rest strokes.

TIP: Listen also for the stronger, warmer, and more uniform tone quality achieved by playing it entirely in second position. Position playing is often used for this purpose, even when it's not needed for reaching notes on the higher frets.

Chorale from *St. Matthew Passion*

J.S. Bach

The melody of this charming piano solo by Schumann is entirely in third position, except for measures 3 and 4, which are in second position. Notice also the open-string B in measure 4; it's used here for convenience in returning to the third-position fingering.

Bagatelle

In this famous Christmas carol, you'll be alternating freely between second- and third-position fingerings beginning at measure 9 (see the *).

TIP: With a bit of practice, you'll find that alternating between second- and third-position fingerings is easy and natural, because it doesn't require an actual position shift. Your thumb only needs to pivot on its tip to support the small back-and-forth hand movement.

God Rest Ye Merry, Gentlemen

19th Century English Carol

Using the Second and Third Position in Solos

A lot of the easy-to-intermediate guitar repertoire is based on first-position playing with occasional use of the higher positions. The next six pieces will introduce you to this kind of music, which requires a somewhat higher level of technique than the music you've played so far.

Gaspar Sanz (1640–1710) was the most important early composer for the Spanish guitar, and several of his pieces have become standards of the concert repertoire. The "Espanoleta" below is also well-known as one of the main themes of Joaquin Roderigo's beautiful guitar concerto "Fantasia Para un Gentilhombre."

✔ **TIP:** In the 1st measure of the second line, be sure to hold down the bass note F for the whole measure.

Espanoleta

Gaspar Sanz

Moderato M.M. ♩ = 120

You've had a lot of practice in bringing out the melody in arpeggiated pieces from the 19th century. The author's composition below shows how the same technique is used to bring out the melody in modern classical guitar music of the same general kind. It also illustrates the fact that sixteenth notes don't necessarily have to be played fast; this is a fairly slow piece with a romantic feel.

✔ **TIP:** In addition to the use of second position in the next to last line of music, notice where the half-barre chord is used.

Prelude in C

Charles Duncan

Lento M.M. ♩ = 58

i m i a i m i

mf

f

poco rit.

mf a tempo

rall.

i m i a

The "Allemande" below is a fine example of the popular Renaissance dance form also spelled as "Alman" or "Aleman"—a stately dance of German origin in 4/4 time.

Likewise, the two transcriptions on the next page are fine examples of one of the most popular Baroque dances, the *Bourree*—a lively dance of French origin in 4/4 time. The composer of the second, Johann Krieger (1651–1735), is not nearly as well-known as J.S. Bach (1685–1750), but several of his pieces for harpsichord also make excellent transcriptions for guitar.

TIP: Each piece uses some unusual position shifting in order to simplify the left-hand requirements. In Bach's "Bourreé," you'll also be playing the note D in the bass line on the *fifth string* where indicated.

Allemande

Anonymous
16th century

Moderato M.M. ♩ = 104

f

mf

i m a m i

f

mf

i m a m i

f

poco rit.

Bourreé

Allegretto M.M. ♩ = 120

J.S. Bach

Bourrée

Allegretto M.M. ♩ = 116

Johann Krieger

"Packington's Pound" is another of the excellent anonymous lute pieces of the Renaissance. Carcassi's "Caprice" on the next page is a light-hearted recreational piece designed to promote the student's technical development.

TIP: In "Caprice," notice the occasional use of the half-barre at the 2nd and 3rd frets. Notice also the 3/8 time signature, which is often used instead of 3/4 for fast pieces in triple meter. Count 3/8 the same way you would count 3/4: "1-and-2-and-3-and," etc.

Packington's Pound

Anonymous
16th century English

Caprice

Matteo Carcassi

Left-Hand Technique: Using Slurs

On the guitar, notes on the same string can be played by the left hand alone. This valuable technique is called **slurring**, and it's used for several purposes:

- ✓ To simplify right-hand fingering and give the plucking fingers a break.
- ✓ To make fast single-note passages easier to play.
- ✓ To make smoother connections between the notes of a melody.
- ✓ To create variety of melodic accent.
- ✓ To produce various kinds of ornaments, also known as **embellishments** (see p. 55).
- ✓ When practiced as exercises, to develop the strength and control of the left hand fingers.

Slurs can be either ascending or descending. Ascending slurs are commonly called **hammer-ons**, while descending slurs are called **pull-offs**. Both are indicated by a **ligature** (i.e., the same kind of short curved line that connects tied notes).

Hammer-On

Pull-Off

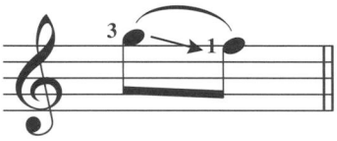

ASCENDING SLURS ("HAMMERING ON")

The common term for ascending slurs, hammer-on, tells you exactly what to do. Pluck the first note, then play the next note by sharply *hammering* your fingertip onto the string. The note is sounded by the percussive impact of the curled fingertip.

TIP: Aim small with your fingertip and try to strike the string just behind the next metal fret—not in the middle of the fret space. This will give you a cleaner-sounding note with less effort.

Practice the following slur exercises on strings 1, 2, and 3 slowly and carefully. Try to produce clean-sounding notes with an even, steady eighth-note rhythm.

DESCENDING SLURS ("PULLING OFF")

The common name for the descending slur, pull-off, also tells you what to do, although a bit more explanation is needed. First, make sure that you're already holding down the second note when you play the first note. Then, to play the second note, pull your fingertip sharply toward the palm of the hand by flexing the tip joint. As you practice the following first-string exercise, remember that you're actually *plucking* the second note with a left-hand finger.

Pull-offs on the lower strings are somewhat trickier, because you have to play the second note without accidentally plucking the next higher string. The best solution to this problem is to pull the fingertip sharply *into* the next higher string, but not across it.

✔ **TIP:** This is basically the same thing that your right-hand fingers do when playing rest strokes.

Practice the following exercises on strings 2 and 3 to develop the fingertip control that you'll need.

Now practice the following second-position exercise that combines strings one, two, and three into a scale pattern of descending slurs.

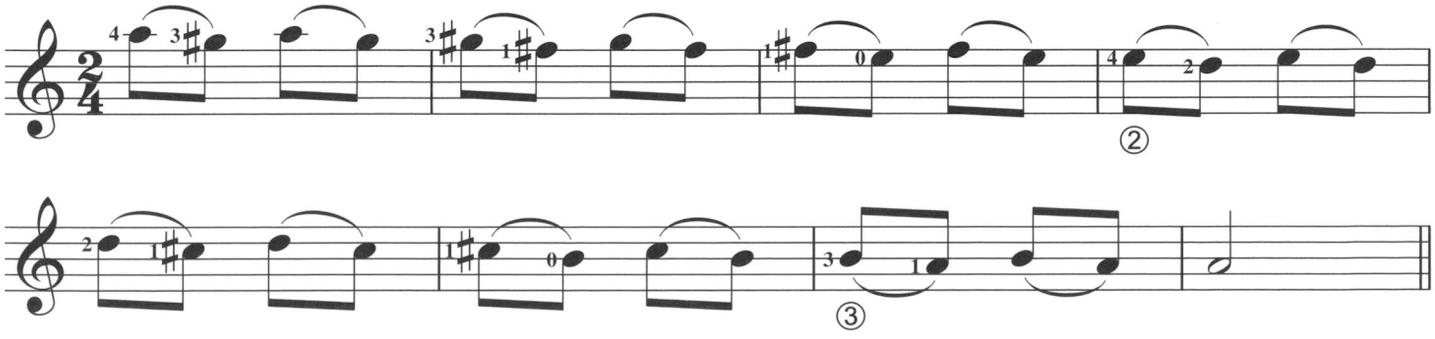

If you can play the preceding exercises, you're ready to play the melody part in the following duets adapted from well-known keyboard pieces. In Bach's "Minuet in G," slurs are used to enhance the rhythmic drive of each group of eighth notes. Slurs are often used for this purpose.

Minuet in G

Jean Philippe Rameau (1683–1764) was a French contemporary of Bach; several of his excellent compositions have also been transcribed for classical guitar. In this one, note the use of slurs to create variety of melodic accent as well as rhythmic drive.

Rondino

The following two pieces by Fabritio Caroso (1527–1605?) will introduce you to the use of slurs in solo playing. Caroso was a composer and dance instructor of the Italian Renaissance; these two pieces are from his dance manual *Il Ballarino* published in 1581.

The first piece is fairly slow and sounds almost like an improvisation. In fact, when played with feeling, it should sound as if you're improvising it yourself. Therefore, you'll need to use slurs only in the first measure of each of the last two lines of music. Here, the slurs will make the execution of the sixteenth notes much easier and more fluent.

Gratia d'Amore

Fabritio Caroso

Andante M.M. ♩ = 88

"Alba Novella" is a faster piece with a stronger beat than "Gratia d' Amore," and therefore slurs can be used to good effect at several points. However, since slurs were not commonly used in lute technique, they are indicated here by the sign for the **optional slur**—a broken ligature: ⌒ You'll see this sign frequently in modern guitar editions of early music, or whenever a modern composer feels that the choice of using the slur should be left up to the player.

✔ **TIP:** Learn the piece without slurs first, then try using them as you're getting the piece up to speed. The closer it approaches the suggested metronome setting, the more natural the slurs will feel and the better they will sound.

Alba Novella

Fabritio Caroso

Allegretto M.M. ♩ = 112

The well-known first section of Beethoven's beautiful piano classic, "Für Elise," makes a very effective guitar solo. Note the optional slurs in the fourth line of music—when you get the piece up to speed, using slurs here will enhance the greater sense of rhythmic urgency conveyed by this section of the piece.

Für Elise

Using Slurs for Ornamentation

Ornamentation (also known as **embellishment**) is the musical term for the decoration or emphasis of a melodic note with rapidly executed notes above and/or below the note. On the guitar, ornaments are usually executed with slurs. You'll learn more about ornamentation in *Book 3*; the last four pieces in this book will introduce you to the use of descending and ascending slurs for ornamentation.

THE GRACE NOTE

The most basic ornament is the **grace note** (𝅘𝅥𝅮), which you play with a *very* quick pull-off. Like most ornaments, it's written as a smaller note connected to the main note with a short ligature. Also like most ornaments, the way it looks can be confusing, especially when the melody note is combined with any lower notes. In all cases, you play the grace note *together with the lower note(s)* and pull off to the main note. The following examples show how grace notes are written and how they are actually played.

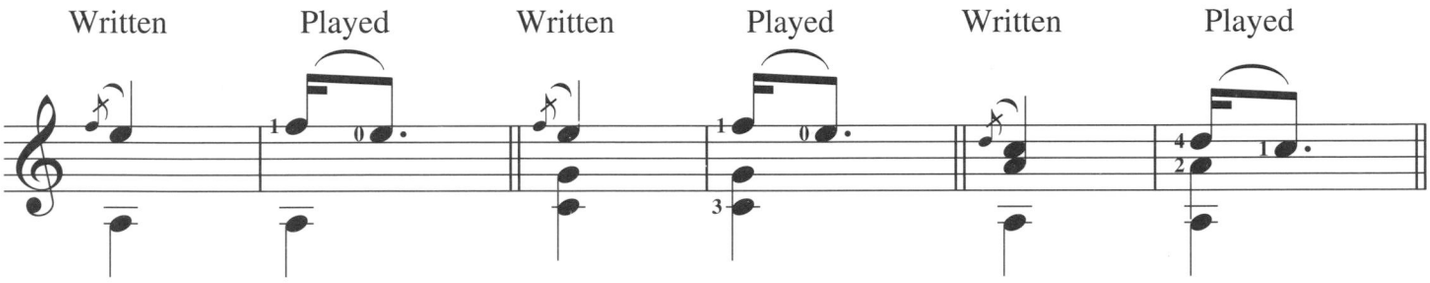

TIP: This ornament tricks the ear. When well played, it sounds as if the main note (not the grace note) falls on the beat. This also helps explain why it's written as a small note before the beat.

THE DOUBLE GRACE NOTE

The **double grace note** takes two forms known as the **mordent** and the **inverted mordent**, shown below. The inverted mordent is more common and is the one we'll be using in the last two pieces. You play it by executing a very quick hammer-on and pull-off, as shown in the second example:

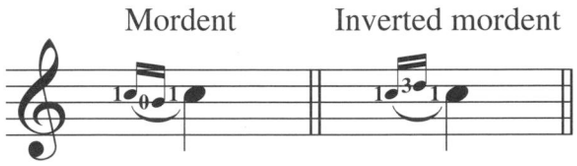

Like the grace note, the first note of this ornament is played together with any lower notes. Also like the grace note, it can sound as if the main note falls on the beat, at least when the music tempo is not very fast. However, as the tempo speeds up, the ornament will sound much more like a triplet:

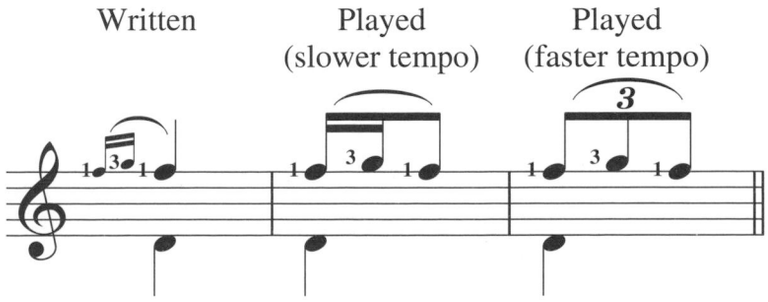

TIP: Just try to execute the double grace note as rapidly as you can. Depending on the tempo of the music, either interpretation of the ornament is perfectly acceptable.

Besides being a very beautiful piece, Sor's "Andante" below provides an easy introduction to playing grace notes. The same grace note is used in the first, second, and fourth lines of music.

In contrast, Giuliani's "Etude" on the next page uses grace notes more extensively, as well as a variety of ascending and descending slurs. This piece is more of a technical challenge, and makes a fine showpiece once you've mastered it.

TIP: Giuliani's "Etude" also introduces a new third-position note: the 6th-fret B♭ on the first string. You'll see it in the last measure of the fourth line of music.

Andante

Fernando Sor

M.M. ♩ = 92

1. 2.

Etude

Mauro Giuliani

Coda: Spanish Music in the Phrygian Mode

A **coda** is a short concluding section at the end of a musical composition. The music symbol is the **coda sign:** 𝄌 As the "coda" to this book, let's look at what makes Spanish music sound "Spanish" and conclude with some Spanish-sounding music.

Modern Spanish music is strongly influenced by the gypsy music called **flamenco**, which is generally based on the **Phrygian mode**. The Phrygian mode is the scale pattern of intervals produced by the A natural minor scale with E (not A) as the root (shown below). When the Phrygian mode is built on any other root, chromatic alteration is needed to keep the pattern of whole steps and half steps the same. (For example, in the common key of A Phrygian, the B must be flatted.)

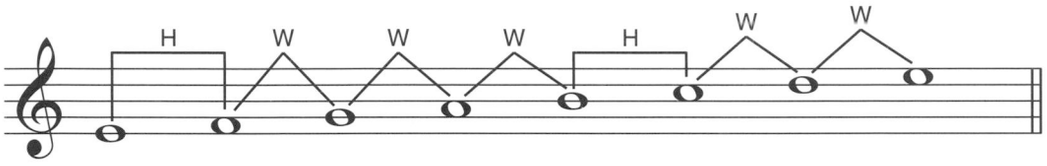

The following Spanish-sounding cadences define the keys of E Phrygian and A Phrygian. Although the other chords are built on the natural minor scale, the tonic chord in Phrygian keys is always major and therefore requires a sharp.

✔ **TIP:** The G, F, and B♭ chords are in the form frequently preferred by flamenco guitarists in order to take advantage of the open strings and create an even more exotic sound.

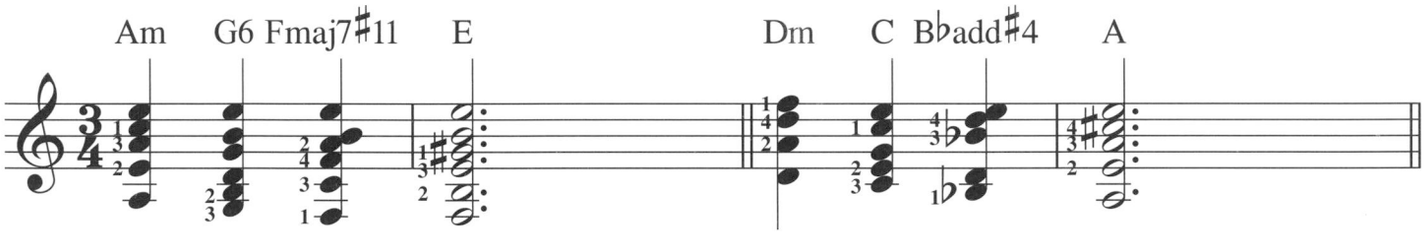

Also, Spanish guitar music often uses the flamenco technique known as **rasgueado**, in which the strings are struck with the back of the fingernails. The most basic rasgueado technique is an up-and-down strum with *i* that's similar to strumming with a guitar pick. Practice using it on the following simple but distinctive flamenco chord progression; the arrows indicate the direction of the strokes.

✔ **TIP:** Notice that, on the upstrokes, you don't need to play all six strings—just four is enough. For downstrokes where the lowest note is on the fifth string, lightly plant your thumb on the sixth string to dampen it.

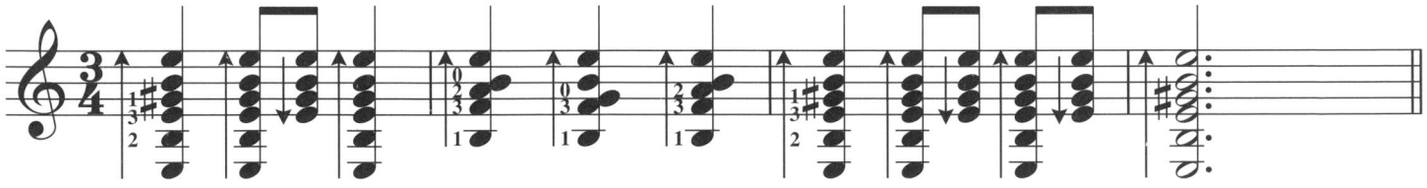

"Fiesta" on the next page, reflects the melodic and harmonic structure of flamenco forms in the key of A Phrygian such as the *bulerias*. Both grace notes and double grace notes are used to embellish the melody, and the piece concludes with a short coda. "Malagueña," on pp. 60–61, is in the key of E Phrygian, and is based on some of the most traditional versions of this famous flamenco dance form. It also uses the same rasgueado chords shown above.

Fiesta

Charles Duncan

Molto Allegro M.M. ♩ = 200

Malagueña

Traditional Flamenco
(arr. Charles Duncan)

p
m
i
a
m
p
f
i m
3
3
3
m i
3
3
3
f
accel.
ff
ff

Appendix: Playing with Fingernails

You'll achieve the best instrumental tone and accuracy by learning to play with your fingernails. Good players vary in the ways that they use their nails, but most of them observe the following basic rules:

- ✓ For all strokes, the string should make simultaneous contact with the nail and the tip of the finger.
- ✓ The fingertip merely "cushions" the nail contact; the actual sound is produced by the nail alone.
- ✓ Even though it only takes a fraction of a second, a fingerstroke has a beginning, middle, and end. Since the quality of tone depends on how smoothly the nail engages the string from contact to release, nails must be filed carefully.
- ✓ Advanced players often vary the contact point to achieve contrasts in tone color. However, for the basic stroke, the contact point is on the left side of the nail (the side nearest the thumb); the release point is slightly past the midpoint of the nail, as shown below.

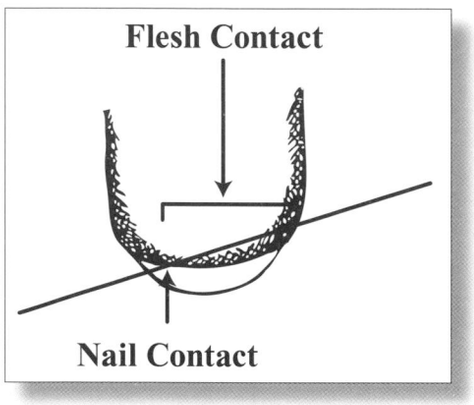

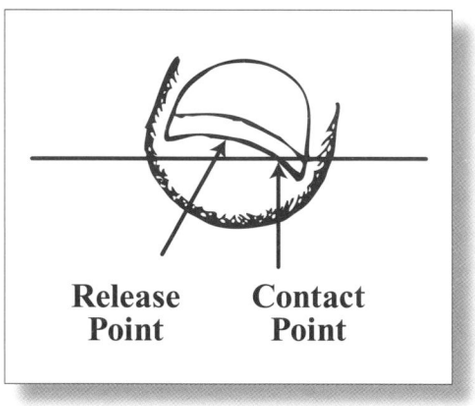

FILING THE NAILS

Various brands of useful nail files are available at nail shops, beauty supply stores, the cosmetics sections of department stores and drugstores, and even dollar stores. Avoid the common metal files; the best ones are made out of synthetic material with surfaces for shaping, smoothing, and polishing. A piece of fine sandpaper (#500 or finer) comes in handy for smoothing off edges, especially from underneath. For final polishing, Open Coat Silicon Carbide Paper is preferred by most players. (Large hardware stores and guitar shops usually carry this paper, and it's also marketed on the internet.)

Shape the nails slowly and carefully with the file at around a 45° angle with the nail. Hold the file steady while you move your fingernail across it with short, gentle back-and-forth strokes. Examine the results frequently from different angles to achieve the correct shape, as shown on the next page.

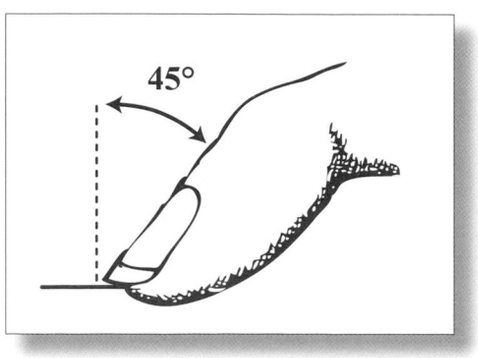

SHAPING THE NAILS

Nails need to be shaped so that they will engage the strings with gentle but firm resistance. Therefore, they should not be long and pointed, but relatively short and blunt. Seen from underneath, as in the first illustration, they should appear 1/16th–1/8th of an inch long. Seen from the side, they should closely resemble the second illustration:

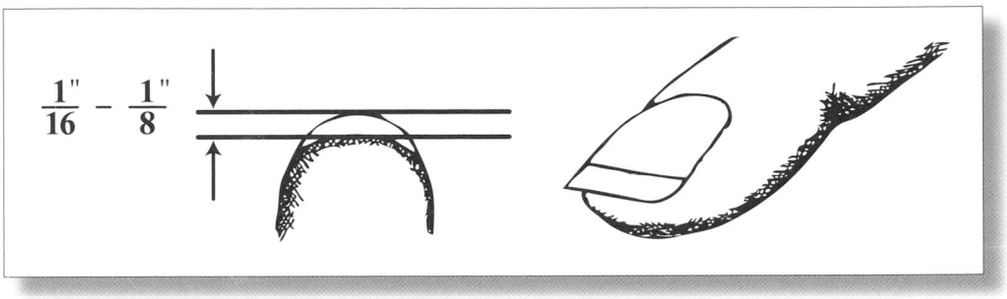

However, in order to get the look of the second illustration, you'll need to adapt the shape to the **arch form** of the nail. Arch form differs from player to player and sometimes between fingers on the same hand. Look closely at your nails head-on, as shown below, to see which arch form they match:

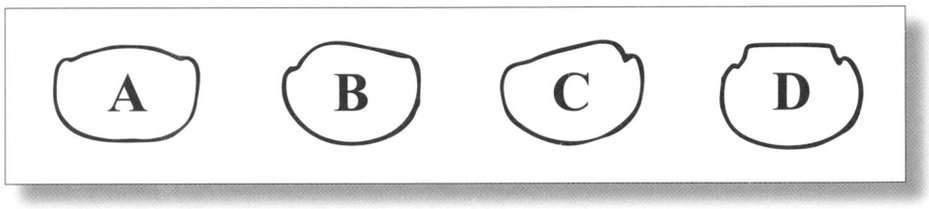

The key to correct shaping is to match the shape (seen from underneath) with the arch form (seen from head-on). In all cases, the peak of the arch is where the nail should appear the longest. If the nail peaks in the middle (arch form A), then the correct shape will be round and symmetrical, just as in the first illustration on this page. If the nail peaks to the left or the right (arch forms B and C), the correct shape will be shown as below:

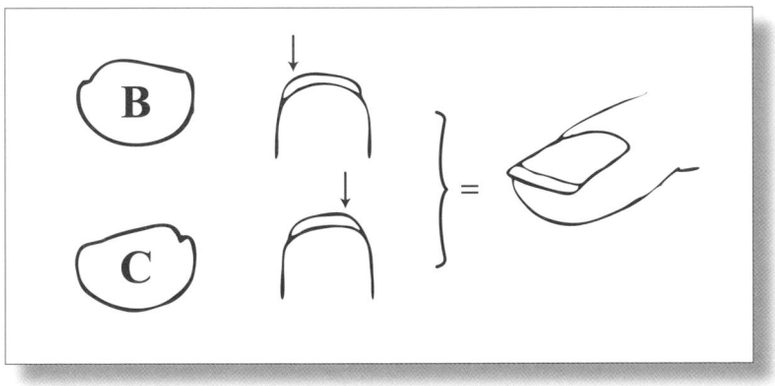

If your nails dip down in the middle as shown below (arch form D), you'll need to file them so that they look flat on the top as seen from underneath:

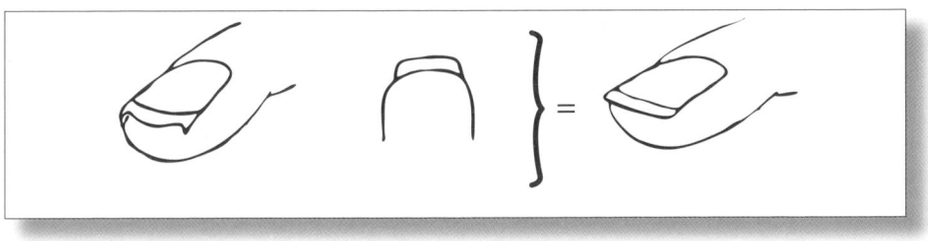

PLAYING WITH THE THUMBNAIL

Good players vary in how they use the thumb. Even the same player will often use different kinds of thumbstrokes consciously or unconsciously to vary the tone. Depending on how you make the nail-to-string contact, there are three kinds of strokes:

1. You can make contact (C) the same way you do for the fingers, close to the edge of the nail, and release (R) at the midpoint (illustration 1)
2. You can make a double-contact at the midpoint and the edge, and release in between them (illustration 2); or
3. You can make contact at the midpoint and release toward the edge (illustration 3).

The *third* option is the one preferred by most players for their basic stroke. However, you should experiment to see which feels best and produces the best tone.

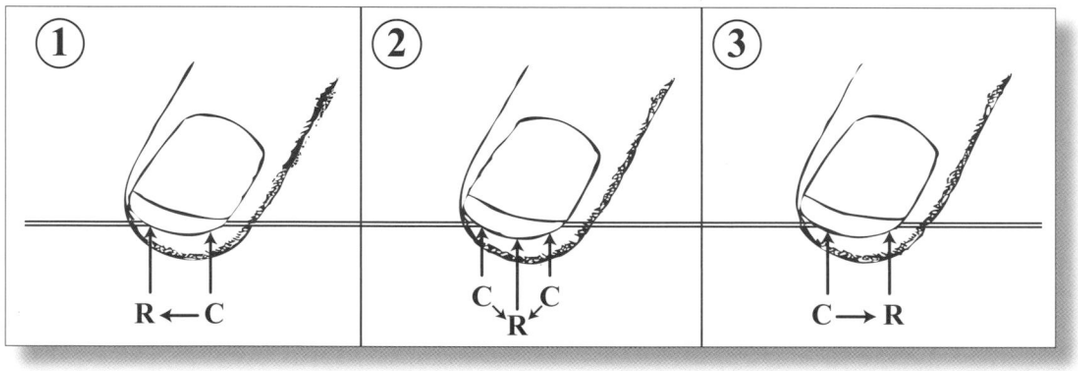

Generally speaking, the thumbnail should be filed according to its arch form just like the fingernails, and should project 1/8–1/4 inch beyond the tip. The relatively greater breadth of the thumb also partly determines the correct nail shape. For a broad thumb with a flattish nail contour, the correct shape will resemble illustration (A); for a somewhat narrower thumb with a more highly arched nail, the correct shape will look more like illustration (B):

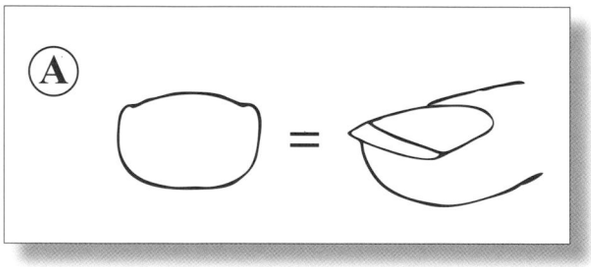

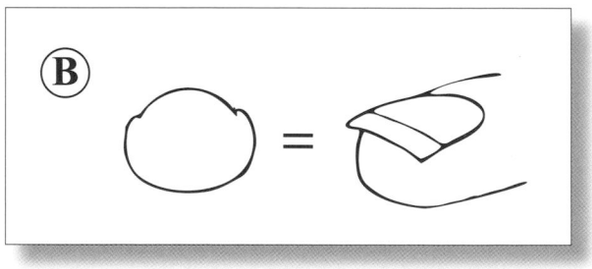

This section will provide you with enough information to start playing with your nails to good advantage. For a more detailed discussion, see Chapter 4 of the author's *The Art of Classical Guitar Playing* (Summy-Birchard Music, 1980), a reference text which continues to be widely used in college and conservative guitar programs.